Neither nor Candle-light

Neither Moon nor Candle-light

Selected Poems of Humbert Wolfe

Chosen by
Ann Wolfe

Edited by
Adam Robbins

With a Foreword by
Louis de Bernières

THE AURIOL PRESS

Published by The Auriol Press in 2002.
5 Auriol Road, London, W14 0SP
adamrobbins@clara.co.uk

Copyright © Ann Wolfe

Foreword © Louis de Bernières
Introduction © Margaret Cunningham

Cover drawing by Sir William Rothenstein RA
Cover design by Olley & Robertson

This book is sold subject to the condition that it shall not, by way of trade or otherwise, be lent, resold, hired out or otherwise circulated without the publisher's prior consent in any form of binding or cover other than that in which it published and without a similar condition being imposed on the subsequent purchaser.

Typeset and printed by Rowland Phototypesetting Ltd,
Bury St Edmunds, Suffolk

ISBN 0-9543511-0-X

Table of Contents

Foreword by Louis de Bernières	ix
Introduction by Margaret Cunningham	xiii
Note on The Text	xvii
Acknowledgements	xvii
Note by Ann Wolfe	xviii

London Sonnets. Oxford 1920.

THE OLD CLOTHES DEALER	1
COVES AT HAMPTON COURT	2
THE FRIED FISH-SHOP	3
THE YORKSHIRE GREY	4
WARDOUR STREET	5
SOMETIMES WHEN I THINK OF LOVE: I.	6
THE SONG OF THE GAMBUCINOS	7
FEBRUARY 14	8

Shylock Reasons with Mr Chesterton, and Other Poems. Oxford 1921.

BATTERSEA	9
A ROOM IN BOHEMIA	10
THE LITTLE SLEEPER (from THREE EPITAPHS)	11
ENVOI	12

Kensington Gardens. London 1924, New York 1927.

Foreword by Ann Wolfe	14
PREFACE	15
TULIP	16
LUPIN	17
LABURNUM	18
THE BLACKBIRD	19
THRUSHES	20
LAMB	21
THE GREY SQUIRREL	22
RACES	23
THE PALACE	24
TAIL-PIECE	25

The Unknown Goddess. London 1925, New York 1925.
ILIAD	26
THE DREAM-CITY	28
OXFORD	30
MY DESK	33
GREEN CANDLES	34
THE FLORAL BANDIT	35
BETELGEUSE	37
THE END	38
IN THE STREET OF LOST TIME	39

Humoresque. London 1926.
PANTALOON	40
From THE STAGE MANAGER	41
THE LAMP IN THE EMPTY ROOM	43
BOY IN THE DUSK	44
NEITHER MOON NOR CANDLE-LIGHT	46
TIMES – MORNING	47
AUTUMN – RESIGNATION	48
DEATH OF HARLEQUINADE	49
THE FOOL HAS SAID IN HIS HEART	51

News of the Devil. London 1926, New York 1926.
War! devil! There is something I remember	53
And now the devil's voice rose up and out	54
EPILOGUE	56

Cursory Rhymes. London 1926, Garden City NY 1928.
INVOCATION	58
PREFACE	59
INTRODUCTION: I	60
INTRODUCTION: II	63
THE BLUECOAT BOY: I	66

Requiem. London 1927, New York 1927.
THE SOLDIER: I	68
THE RESPECTABLE WOMAN: I	69
THE TEACHER: II	71

THE UNCOMMON MAN: I	72
CODA - THE HIGH SONG	73

This Blind Rose. London 1928, Garden City NY 1929.

THE HOUSE OF GHOSTS	74
THIS BLIND ROSE	75
A LITTLE MUSIC	76
MOUNTAIN-FLOWERS	78
MY POEMS	79
GENEVA – I. RUE DU SOLEIL LEVANT	81
SPRING WOOD	82
NOW IN THESE FAIRYLANDS	83

The Uncelestial City. London 1930, New York 1930.

Do you know Blackford? Nature keeps the tally	84
If I had money, as I have none,	85
You cannot hope	87
The primrose on	88
Eve heard you singing,	89
The House of Lords	90
Up and down Pall Mall, and then	91
Agamemnon sleeps at last in Argos.	92
When all the London boys begin	93
I think there must be some	94
You can fool life perhaps at twenty-one,	96
It is easier to be angrier than to pity,	97
Pausing in her cool affairs,	99

X at Oberammergau: A Poem London 1935.

Fades now the star, and, by their camels kneeling	100
He has gone down to death. Cease, women, your sorrow.	101

The Upward Anguish. London 1938.

From CHAPTER I: SCHOLARSHIP JOURNEY	102

Out of Great Tribulation. London 1939.
AT THE END OF THE AVENUE	106
THE LIGHT-FOOTED	107
THE SNOW-DICTATED PEACE	108
TWO OBOLS	109
RED SHOES	110
I PRAISE OTHER WOMEN	111
HOLLINGS HILL	112
ANOTHER WAY	113
CONVERSATION GALLANTE	115
KING AND CAT	117
EPITAPH	118

Kensington Gardens in War-time. (posthumously) London 1940.
VI	119
VIII	120
XV	121
XVI	122
XVII	123
XX	124
XXX	125

Index of First Lines	127

Foreword by Louis de Bernières

I first came across the poetry of Humbert Wolfe by happy accident, thanks to my habit of browsing in second-hand bookshops. I am always hoping to discover forgotten poets, and on this occasion I spotted a slight volume entitled *Requiem*. It fell open on page 31, and there was a poem so unmistakeably excellent that I bought the book for forty pence, feeling almost like a thief. That poem was 'The Soldier', and I used it at the beginning of my fourth novel (*Captain Corelli's Mandolin*) because its puzzled rhetoric captured exactly the questions raised for me by the massacre of thousands of young Italians on Cephallonia in 1943. It also had a personal reverberation, because it is a reflection upon the protracted ordeal endured by my grandfather and his comrades in the Great War. My grandfather committed suicide in the 1960s, at least partly because of the appalling physical legacy of his war wounds. Everybody who read 'The Soldier' was struck by the quality of the poem, but no-one had heard of Humbert Wolfe.

As time went by, however, I began to receive letters from older readers who wished to express their delight. Characteristically they would write something like 'I have always loved his poetry, but I thought I was the only one who still remembered him.' One old lady, Christina Beardmore, of Brighton, sent me her copy of *The Uncelestial City*, which she had acquired in December 1939, with an accompanying note that said, 'I have been thinking for some time I would send you one of my HWs if only to ensure it a good home, so here it is…' I was very moved by the thought that a book of verse might have provoked such special affection and loyalty in its owner that she would wish to give it a long future in safe hands.

The reader will here discover poems which are urban and poems that are rural, poems that are epigrammatic, poems about the sorrow of war, poems that remind one of Auden, poems that are passionate but restrained, poems that are decidedly anachronistic (because of the use of apostrophe, quite often), and poems which are thoroughly modern. One is struck most frequently by Wolfe's sense of loss, resignation, and regret. He is disappointed by the ordinariness of life, but most of all he is preoccupied by what used to be called 'mutabilitie'. Everything is changeable, unreliable, ephemeral. Everything comes to an end:

> ...all passion
> is nothing made
> but a star to flash in
> an Iliad.

One feels that Wolfe must have struggled much with the melancholy that attaches itself to the apprehension of futility. His poetry is thoughtful rather than bitter, however, and he celebrates often enough, with enough wit and affection, to leave the reader in an even frame of mind. It should also be pointed out that all his verse is very carefully structured and crafted; there is never any sign of it being the kind of distorted or dismembered prose that only comes to resemble poetry when read aloud in a portentous or otherwise idiosyncratic tone of voice. This is a satisfaction in itself, albeit an old-fashioned one.

The greater proportion of poets certainly deserve to be forgotten. This is as true now as it has always been, and one ought to be intelligently sceptical of the romantic notion that literary history is bursting at the seams with unacknowledged geniuses. There is such a thing as literary fashion, however, bringing with it all the disgusting intellectual snobbery that this entails, and I would suggest that there are quite a number of poets who have been all but lost to us because of the superciliousness of the modernists who managed to set themselves up as the kings of the castle. Rupert Brooke, for example, has never received due recognition for the quality of his love poetry, and John Masefield's sonnets need to be reread. We may or may not ultimately decide that we cannot like the verse of Kipling, Walter de la Mare, W.H. Davies, or Thomas Hardy, but we should at least have consulted their work before so deciding. Humbert Wolfe is another one of the many who deserve a new crack of the whip, because amid the hundreds of workmanlike or merely 'good' poems that he produced, there really are some small masterpieces. His daughter, Ann, has chosen for this volume the poems that have the most resonance for her, and no doubt I, or Christina Beardmore of Brighton, would have chosen differently. The important point is that at last Wolfe's boat is to be relaunched. Perhaps his work may begin to turn up in anthologies, and perhaps one day there will be a volume of Complete Verse to do him proper honour.

Louis de Bernières, 1999

Introduction

Humbert Wolfe was born in Milan in 1885 of Jewish parents. They settled in Bradford, where his father, Martin, became the owner of a warehouse, but died when his son was eleven. Wolfe tells us in his autobiographical work, *Now a Stranger*, that he could remember his father only as an invalid in the background. He was brought up by his mother Consola, in a large family of children: an elder brother who was his childhood hero, and three sisters. His mother was not religious, but he was sent to the Jewish Sunday School which bored him besides exposing him to taunts of 'Allo, Jew-boy' and 'Oo killed Christ' on the way home. Wolfe was baptised as a Christian just before marriage and told his fiancée that he had been converted by Cranmer's English in the *Book of Common Prayer*. He never became an orthodox Christian, and was always conscious of his own Jewishness and of the injustices suffered by his fellow Jews.

He was educated at Bradford Grammar School, winning a scholarship to Wadham College, Oxford, where he took a First in Greats in 1907. *The Upward Anguish* shows that his special interest was in philosophy.

In 1910 he married Jessie Chalmers Graham, the daughter of a Scottish schoolmaster. They had first met on a beach near Oban, when Jessie, aged about ten, was suddenly accosted by a small boy of eight with the request, 'May we borrow your big spade?'. After this there were occasional meetings, and Berto (the name his family always called him) used sometimes to send poems to Jessie. Their engagement was sparked off in Berto's final year at Oxford when Jessie and a friend called on him in his college room. He recalls this in his dedication to *Requiem*, a sequence of poems: 'To my visitor on No. 10 staircase at Wadham College'. The marriage, as Ann, his only surviving child, remembers it, was a stormy one, full of 'love's quarrellings and love's renewals'.

In 1908 he joined the Civil Service where he worked up until his sudden death on his birthday, January 5, 1940, in the first months of World War II. His work there was greatly valued and he was appointed C.B.E in 1918 and C.B. in 1925. In 1938 he was made Deputy Secretary at the Ministry of Labour, and in 1939 he played an important part in raising a million men and women for civil defence, defying doctor's orders to do so at the cost of his own life.

His personal political views went through several dramatic changes. In *The Upward Anguish* he describes the active part he played in Conservative politics in his later undergraduate years, and when war broke out he tried everything he knew to get permission to enlist, but was rejected because of a serious heart defect. But around 1924 he startled his family at election time by suddenly announcing, 'I shall vote Labour', and then for a time he adopted the outright pacifism then common in the Labour Party. 'All wars and all their dead have been the same', he wrote in *The Uncelestial City*.

However, when Hitler's outrages on the Jews became known he was among the first to denounce him, and wrote his drama, *X at Oberammergau*, portraying Christ crucified again at the Passion Play because he acknowledged that he was a Jew.

In spite of his busy life as a Civil Servant, he found time to become well known as a writer, a reviewer and a brilliant and witty public speaker. He covered a wide field, especially literary criticism, particularly of poetry and wrote prefaces to editions of Herrick and Shelley, and a penetrating study of Tennyson. His criticism of contemporary writers was often controversial, but always interesting, brilliantly expressed and shot through with his individual sense of humour.

He also wrote several autobiographical works. These include *Now a Stranger*, which gives vivid glimpses of his life in Bradford between the ages of five and nine, and *The Upward Anguish*, a brilliant satirical picture of his undergraduate years at Oxford.

But Wolfe's great longing was to be a poet. 'Prose,' he wrote in his Introduction to *A Winter Miscellany*, 'is all apples to me—von Koppen's apples I mean, sour potatoes.' Beginning with a school poem published in *The Bradfordian*—a lament for the last steam tram from Bradford to Saltaire—he published a number of volumes of poetry, including many verse translations of Greek, German and especially French poetry. His works often ran to several editions. The composer Gustav Holst chose twelve of his poems to set to music for piano and soprano voice.

In *P.L.M. People, Landfalls, Mountains* (an account of a convalescing holiday in France) Wolfe describes a conversation with 'a pale young man' in a hotel at Lautaret. The young man asked him for help with the English of a poem, 'Autumn', which he had found quoted in Maurois' *Disraeli*; Wolfe admitted that he knew the verses '"well, because I wrote them'… 'You are then, Monsieur, a poet.' 'As to that,' I replied, 'it is for others to judge, and, to be honest the majority of my English critics do not think so. But at least I love poetry better than life, and seek to write it.'"

Ann and I have made a selection of our favourite poems and added some prose extracts. We think the best of them are too good to be forgotten, and also that some of them, especially, I think, 'Mr Emmanuel Crayfish' (an extract from the beginning of *The Uncelestial City*), have now become interesting as 'period pieces'.

Margaret L. Cunningham

Note on the text

My 'editorial' contribution to this volume has been a technical one. The poems were chosen by Ann Wolfe and my mission, or rather, my privilege, has simply been to publish and give life to her selection as accurately and attractively as possible.

Apart from correcting occasional glaring typographical errors, I have faithfully reproduced the texts of the poems in their originally published format. Any idiosyncrasies of punctuation or structure are therefore Wolfe's, any errors are my own.

Footnotes have been written by Margaret Cunningham (MC) and Ann Wolfe (AW).

Adam Robbins

Acknowledgements

The editorial team has greatly appreciated the contribution of a whole host of professional colleagues, friends and relations. Words of encouragement and technical publishing advice have mercifully been in plentiful supply, and we would in particular like to thank:

Philip Bagguley, Ann Barefoot, Guy Barefoot, Melanie Bhagat, Jill Boothroyd, Hannah Casey, Sandy Dutczak, Simon Harper, Fiona MacDonald, Kate Mervyn Jones, Stuart Millar, Daniel Robbins, Keith Robbins and Anna Thomson.

Note

For more information, please refer to the biography *A Harlequin at Whitehall: A Life of Humbert Wolfe, Poet and Civil Servant, 1885-1940* by Philip Bagguley (London, 1997).

Humbert Wolfe published fourteen volumes of poetry (apart from translations) between 1920 and 1940. Some of the poems in my selection have a personal link, others have simply chosen themselves by their wit and irony, their humanity, sense of the 'tears of things', a feeling of reality, a sense of mystery, and sometimes pure magic.

Ann Wolfe

THE OLD CLOTHES DEALER

It's not my fault, now is it? I'm a Jew.
  I'd a been born a Christian quick enough
  If only so I could have sold my stuff
Double the price, and not be called a screw.
There's half-day Saturday at Synagogue,
  And when Atonement comes a whole day lost.
  O, I don't grumble; still one counts the cost
When on the top I'm treated like a dog.
And, though a Jew shouldn't by rights complain
  Bein' the chosen, can't a man have dreams?
  Clothes' dealing's not the desert, still it seems
We all of us are wandering again.
I often think when the Shemah begins
"O God o' Jacob ain't we paid our sins?"

COVES AT HAMPTON COURT

You go by motor-bus from Hammersmith
   And come back loud and cheerful after dark
   Adorned with twigs you've plucked in Bushey Park,
Eating the sandwiches you started with.
And you don't care, why should you? when you're brought
   Into the grimy streets out of the green,
   That, if you'd had the luck, you might have been
The sort of cove who lives at Hampton Court.

You've got the murders and the betting news,
   And slums to bake in and the picture shows.
   Why should you care if somewhere a red rose
Burns all night through, and the great avenues
Are lit as though with candles. What's the odds?
London's for you; the summer's for the gods.

THE FRIED FISH-SHOP

The upper clawses they don't like the smell
   Nor they don't need to. They can pay for food,
   But we who sometimes cawn't, it does us good.
Lord, what a life to 'ave fried fish to sell!
Warm all day long and nuthin' much to do
   And always a hot bit if you're inclined.
   Shut all day Sundays and if you've a mind
Always go out and pitch into a Jew.
But wanting won't mend 'oles up in your socks
   Nor cure that 'ungry feeling when you stands
   Clappin' your stummick with your empty 'ands
And thinking gently of a wooden box
Where they will lay you at the parish charge
   Straight if you're small and doubled if you're large.

THE YORKSHIRE GREY

The Yorkshire Grey like any other pub,
  Quietly blazes till the final shout
  "Time's-up" sends the companions tumbling out,
Giving their lips a last reluctant rub.
And if you're passing by on any day
  You'll hear a woman with a barrel organ,
  Sing in a high cracked voice what sounds like "Morgen,
Morgen kommt nie und heute is mir weh,"
And every day whether it's rain or shine
  She holds an old umbrella with a handle
  Of curiously carved silver. Whether scandal
Or tragedy, it's no affair of mine.
Why should I care then when some drunken feller
Sends her to blazes, her and her umbrella.

WARDOUR STREET

There's a small cafe off the Avenue
   Where Alphonse, that old sinner, used to fix
   A five-course dinner up at one and six,
And trust to luck and youth to pull him through.
I can't remember much about the wine
   Except that it was ninepence for the quart
   Called claret and was nothing of the sort,
Cheap like the rest and like the rest divine.
But Alphonse, I suppose, is long since sped
   And madame's knitting needles rusted through
   And even Marguerite, like us she flew
To wait on, waited on by death instead.
Well Alphonse, well Madame, well Marguerite
They've no more use for us in Wardour Street.

"SOMETIMES WHEN I THINK OF LOVE"

I.

Sometimes when I think of love
I think of Mimi singing in Boheme,
Just as the tune across the footlights came
When we were young, my dear, at Covent Garden!
Poor music, but before the senses harden
Puccini's made for boys and girls to wear
Spite of sham passion and a poitrinaire.
For if they looked and didn't find the key
At least they found the hearts of you and me.
That sort of love age thinks of with a smile
How innocent it was of truth and guile,
How young perhaps and yet how half-divine
And how imperishably yours and mine.
You will not wonder nor will you reprove
My thoughts of Mimi when I think of love.

THE SONG OF THE GAMBUCINOS

The little houses in the street
  And the warm blinds at night,
Outside the copper on his beat
  And the moon so white, so white.

They know what we shall never know,
  See what we cannot see,
The steady lamplit ways that go
  To the quiet cemetery.

They have not any fear at all
  Of life and of its end.
They hear church bells, their children call,
  Their wife and death their friend.

But for us the moon is white, so white
  It drowns us and it stings,
And we must fly throughout the night
  Because of dangerous things.

Note
Gambucinos: possibly some sort of gypsies. I remember my mother saying that my father thought our family were like the Gambucinos, always outside, looking in. AW.

FEBRUARY 14

Let's be done with talking,
  Words are half a snare,
That fools use for stalking
  What was never there.

Let's be done with weeping,
  Tears are but a sign
That a doom is creeping
  On what was divine.

Why be broken-hearted?
  Time to break the heart
If we should be parted
  And not care we part.

Dear, the wind is over
  In the world outside.
I was once your lover,
  You were once my bride.

Let's go out together.
  In the quiet air,
We may find each other
  Waiting as we were.

BATTERSEA

I have always known just where the river ends
(Or seems to end) that I shall find my friends,
Who are my friends no longer, being dead,
And hear the ordinary things they said,
That now seem wonderful, some evening when
I take the Number Nineteen bus again
To Battersea. It will, I think, be clear
With stars behind the four great chimneys. Dear
In the moon, young and unchanging, they
Will cry me welcome in the boyish way
They had before they went to France, but I,
A boy no more, will greet them silently.

Note
When Wolfe published an edition of his early poems in 1930, he singled out this poem in his preface, as one where he could 'find nothing that he should wish to change'. MC.

A ROOM IN BOHEMIA

The sun is shining in the August weather
  In the little room and, I suppose,
Gilding the painted parrot on the wall,
  The truckle-bed, the table and the rose
Of the poor carpet that we bought together.
  And from the street the muted voices call
  As though we saw, as though we heard it all.

From THREE EPITAPHS

III. THE LITTLE SLEEPER

This little sleeper, who was overtaken
  By death, as one child overtakes another,
Dreams by his side all night and will not waken
    Till the dawn comes in heaven with his mother.

ENVOI

Past Buckhurst Hill the motor-bus
Takes and shakes the three of us.
When first we went, there were but two
In Epping Forest, I and you.

That summer as I understand
A forester from fairyland
Set a notice up, "No road,"
By the ways our feet had trod.

No one came and no one knew,
When the spring returned and blue
Flowers burned, how deep behind
Burned the blossoms of the mind.

No one guessed and no one heard
How beyond the singing bird,
Some one sang in solitude
In the wood within the wood.

No one watched the years go by
(Not even you, not even I),
In the wood alone apart
Green and waiting in the heart.

Till last week the forester
Heard a little footstep stir,
Took his notice down and smiled
At the coming of a child.

Conquering the solitude
A child is laughing in the wood.
Past Buckhurst Hill the motor-bus
Takes us back the three of us.

Note
There was a picnic in Epping Forest. We sat on a tree-trunk and ate our lunch which included hard-boiled eggs that weren't! AW.

KENSINGTON GARDENS

When I was a child we lived in a flat near Kensington Gardens. We had no garden, so Kensington Gardens did instead and became part of our life.

One brilliant May in 1923, when I was rising ten, my father and I used to walk in the Gardens every morning before breakfast.

We would come back down Church Street, past the Belgian bakery, and I would go in to ask for "Huit croissants s'il vous plaît", to be taken back, hot and fresh, to my mother for breakfast.

Afterwards my father would leave for the Ministry of Labour in Whitehall. In the evening I'd watch for him coming back along Kensington High Street from the Underground.

Later, perhaps, supposedly in bed, I might glimpse him from the stairs, writing at his desk in the yellow glow of the reading-lamp, a tin of ginger nuts beside him.

Next spring he gave me a copy of Kensington Gardens with this inscription:

Ann's Book
from
the person who
copied it out[†]
with love
Feb 18/24

AW.

[†] *i.e. Daddy*

PREFACE

Into spring
,whispering
"O," there ran
my daughter Ann.

TULIP

Clean as a lady
,cool as glass,
fresh without fragrance
the tulip was.

The craftsman, who carved her
of metal, prayed:
"Live, oh thou lovely!"
Half metal she stayed.

LUPIN

Said the old deaf gardener
"I'm wore out with stoopin'
over them impident
sword-blue lupin.

Look at 'em standing
, as cool as kings,
and me sopped to the middle
with bedding the things."

Note
All the lupins we saw then were blue. The many-coloured Russell lupins had not yet reached Kensington Gardens. AW.

LABURNUM

Laburnum hangs
her golden fleece
through a thousand
lattices.

In the silken
flosses caught
struggles spring,
the Argonaut.

THE BLACKBIRD

In the far corner
, close by the swings,
every morning
a blackbird sings.

His bill's so yellow,
his coat's so black,
that he makes a fellow
whistle back.

Ann, my daughter,
thinks that he
sings for us two
especially.

THRUSHES

The City Financier
walks in the gardens
, stiffly, because of
his pride and his burdens.

The daisies, looking
up, observe
only a self-
respecting curve.

The thrushes only
see a flat
table-land
of shiny hat.

He looks importantly
about him,
while all the spring
goes on without him.

LAMB

The old bellwether
looked at the lamb,
as a gentleman looks
when he mutters "Damn!"

"If you jump and frisk,
you little fool,
you'll only end
by losing your wool.

When I was a lamb
I always would
behave as like a sheep
as I could."

"Did you!" the lamb
replied with a leap,
"I always thought
You were born a sheep."

The park-keeper said
to the boy on the fence
"Let's have less
of your impudence!

Off with you now,
and do as you're bade,
or you'll end in prison.
When I was a lad ..."

THE GREY SQUIRREL

Like a small grey
coffee-pot
sits the squirrel.
He is not

all he should be,
kills by dozens
trees, and eats
his red-brown cousins.

The keeper, on the
other hand
, who shot him, is
a Christian, and

loves his enemies,
which shows
the squirrel was not
one of those.

RACES

Alf and Betty
are having a race
with little Jim
in the packing-case.

Off comes a wheel,
out sprawls Jim.
"I'd 'ave won," says Betty,
"except for 'im."

Note
I saw this happen. AW.

THE PALACE

The gold cock-pheasant
they tell me, Ann,
is by extraction
        Indian.

(What is extraction?
It's a word
meaning, girls should be
seen not heard.)

When he bends down,
he looks for prints
of secret tigers
striped like chintz;

he fears the cool
long cobras, when
he clutters warnings
to his hen;

and the calm English
lawn, and this
most English of
all palaces

are lily lawns
round what they call
(I don't know why!)
the Taj Mahal;

and, if we understood
his shrieks,
we'd find he took
us two for Sikhs.

TAIL-PIECE

"Out! All out!"
Harsh echoes blow
from far. With wandering steps
and slow
once again their
garden leave
little Adam
little Eve.

ILIAD

False dreams, all false,
mad heart, were yours.
The word, and nought else,
in time endures.
Not you long after,
perished and mute,
will last, but the defter
viol and lute,
Sweetly they'll trouble
the listeners
with the cold dropped pebble
of painless verse.
Not you will be offered,
but the poet's false pain.
Mad heart, you have suffered,
and loved in vain.
What joy doth Helen
or Paris have
where these lie still in
a nameless grave?
Her beauty's a wraith,
and the boy Paris
muffles in death
his mouth's cold cherries.
Aye! these are less,
that were love's summer,
than one gold phrase
of old blind Homer?
Not Helen's wonder
nor Paris stirs,
but the bright untender
hexameters.

And thus, all passion
is nothing made,
but a star to flash in
an Iliad.
Mad heart, you were wrong!
No love of yours,
but only what is sung,
when love's over, endures.

Note
In this poem Wolfe must be following up Helen's words to Hector. Iliad VI 355-8: "No one in Troy has a greater burden to bear than you, all through me, shameless bitch that I am, and the reckless wickedness of Paris, us two, on whom Zeus laid an evil doom that we might figure in the songs of those who are yet to be born." MC.

THE DREAM-CITY

On a dream-hill we'll build our city,
and we'll build gates that have two keys—
love to let in the vanquished, and pity
to close the locks that shelter these.

There will be quiet open spaces,
and shady towers sweet with bells,
and quiet folks with quiet faces,
walking among these miracles.

There'll be a London Square in Maytime
with London lilacs, whose brave light
startles with coloured lamps the daytime,
with sudden scented wings the night.

A silent Square could but a lonely
thrush on the lilacs bear to cease
his song, and no sound else—save only
the traffic of the heart at peace.

And we will have a river painted
with the dawn's wistful stratagems
of dusted gold, and night acquainted
with the long purples of the Thames.

And we will have—oh yes! the gardens
Kensington, Richmond Hill and Kew,
and Hampton, where winter scolds, and pardons
the first sweet crocus breaking through.

And where the great their greatness squander,
and while the wise their wisdom lose,
squirrels will leap, and deer will wander,
gracefully, down the avenues.

Note
This poem was set to music by Gustav Holst in 1929. Imogen Holst, in her introduction to *Twelve Sonnets Set to Music by Gustav Holst,* (Galliard Ltd, Norfolk), writes "they [Holst and Wolfe] both enjoyed solitary walks through London at any hour of the day or night, knowing that they would find long stretches where they could be as quiet as in the country. The poem called The Dream City, which was the first my father set to music, gives the impression that it might have been specially written for him. The parts of London that it mentions - the river, Kensington Gardens, Richmond Hill and Kew - had provided him with his favourite walks for more than thirty years."

OXFORD

Some day I'll go back to Oxford—
I shall take the 4-50 from Paddington
(or its sweet ghost if it has ceased to run).
The porter will smile at my waistcoat and my ways,
when I'm not looking, as he used to in other days,
when I thought I was a man about town, and would stand
no nonsense, and he, I suppose, sniggered behind his hand.
I shall sit in my first-class carriage (Everyone
travels first class to Oxford from Paddington,
except the Rhodes scholars, who never can
realize the responsibility of being an Oxford man).
At first I shall read without a trace of feeling,
and indicate a suitable contempt for Acton and Ealing.
I shall light a cigar, extremely black and thick
(and pray inwardly that it won't make me sick!)
And I shall languidly read over again
the latest speech of Mr. Joseph Chamberlain.
I'll nod my head in careless assent to gall
the man in the corner, who looks like a Radical,
(If he isn't why does he get
stuff like "The Star," "The Morning Leader" and
  "The Westminster Gazette."
I can understand giving the other side a chance,
but damn it! there are limits to tolerance!)

Then if I find that my acting is going badly,
and the old chap doesn't notice me, I'll take down Bradley,
and pretend to enjoy the "Ethics," and show the old fool
that, whatever he may be feeling, I am cool.
And that my blood doesn't jump like a fish, and shiver
with a soft deep sucking movement, into the river,

that I can just see, looking furtively sideways,
sweeping into the evening with haunted tideways,
and hidden under the woods that belt and crown it
with one white swan or two dream-floating down it.

I shall look perfectly calm, if anything calmer
than before, when we pass the works of Messrs. Huntley
  and Palmer.
And, while my heart will be wild like a groom at his
  wedding,
when the bride lifts her veil, I'll merely mutter
  "Reading"
(And if the man in the corner looks up suddenly,
as though there was something that stirred his heart in me,
as though he guessed, and saw, and understood
how young I was, how glad, and found it good,
even though the fated end of boyhood, dim
with a brief beauty, clothed me, I'll strangle him.)

Didcot at last, Radley, and then still stiffly
(because perhaps he's watching) I'll look for Iffley.
Then I'll forget how old I am, and how wise,
and how remote from anything in the way of ecstasies,
because I shall see, like frozen lily-flowers
planted by a stone gardener of dreams, the Oxford towers.

I shall step out silently, and take a cab,
that slides along the cobbles like a wounded crab.
I'll say to the cabman "Wadham," and then sit
perfectly still, but my body will be lit
like a great house with candles. While I stare
steadily before me as though I didn't care.

Until we rattle up the Broad and clatter
into Parks Road. And nothing then will matter.

The college windows will be lit, and someone will shout:
"Good Lord! here's Wolfe again," and I'll get out,
and pass through the college gateway into the Quad.
Some day I'll go back to Oxford.

MY DESK

All that I ask
is a desk—
with blotting paper white
changed every night;
no litter but the good
company of cool wood;
a glass inkpot so clean
my pen can wade therein
up to her waist and not
be liable to blot—
also laid in her place
a crystal pencil-case;
and in that glassy bed—
pencils new sharpened;
nothing to vex the soul
in the neat pigeon-hole;
and finally there must
be not a speck of dust.

And I would have the wall
austerely virginal,
with nothing to intervene
(above my desk) between
the thing I try to see
and me.

There let me sit
and write at it—
content with this
slim doorway to infinities.

GREEN CANDLES

"There's someone at the door," said gold candlestick
"Let her in quick, let her in quick!"
"And little fingers faltering at the handle.
Why don't you turn it?" asked green candle.

"Don't go, don't go" said the Hepplewhite chair
"lest you find a strange lady there!"
"Yes! stay where you are" whispered the white wall
"there is nobody there at all".

"I know her little foot" grey carpet said
"Who but I should know her light tread?"
"She shall come in" answered the open door
"and not" said the room "go out any more".

Note
The child fumbling at the door was me. I remember that grey carpet. It had a border of red lines, suitable tracks for my toy tram. AW.

THE FLORAL BANDIT

Beyond the town—oh far! beyond it
   she walks - that lady - have you seen her?
that thief of spring, that floral bandit
   who leaves the grass she walks on greener.

And she can sing—the blackbirds hear her
   —those little coals with throats of flame—
and they can find, alighting near her,
   no sweeter practice than her name.

What is her name? O ask the linnet,
   for human tongue would strive in vain
to speak the buds uncrumpling in it,
   and the small language of the rain.

Who is this lady? What is she?
   the Sylvia all our swains adore?
Yes, she is that—unchangingly,
   but she is also something more.

For buds at best are little green
   keys on an old thin clavichord,
that only has the one high tune
   that, since the first, all springs have heard.

And all first love with the same sighing,
   tunes, though more sweetly touched, has lingered,
as though he were for ever trying
   toccatas Purcell might have fingered.

But no one knows her range, nor can
  guess half the phrases of her fiddle,
the lady who for every man
  breaks off her music in the middle.

Note
This poem was set to music by Gustav Holst in 1929.

BETELGEUSE

    On Betelgeuse
the gold leaves hang in golden aisles
for twice a hundred million miles,
and twice a hundred million years
they golden hang, and nothing stirs,
    on Betelgeuse.

Space is a wind that does
not blow on Betelgeuse,
and time - oh time - is a bird,
whose wings have never stirred
the golden avenues
of leaves on Betelgeuse.

    On Betelgeuse
there is nothing that joys or grieves
the unstirred multitude of leaves,
nor ghost of evil or good
haunts the gold multitude
    on Betelgeuse.

And birth they do not use
nor death on Betelgeuse,
and the God, of whom we are
infinite dust, is there
a single leaf of those
gold leaves on Betelgeuse.

Note

Among my father's books, there was a school-prize - Ball's 'Astronomy'. I read this with interest, and pestered him with questions. One day he produced this poem, about the great red star in Orion, as an answer. AW. This poem was set to music by Gustav Holst in 1929.

THE END

When the house of the heart is empty,
   and the thin dust,
like snow, begins to settle:
   and, red as rust,

the sun comes in by the window
   at the broken pane,
till night with her blackened dishcloth
   stops it up again.

Then up the carpetless staircase
   drag their slippered feet
the dead days, and the dead desires—
   shuffle and pass and meet.

Downstairs in the cellar the darkness
   is deep enough to swim in,
and, there, washing back and forwards
   are pale men, and pale drowned women.

The friends no longer quarrel,
   the lovers do not kiss—
and one day, or the other day
   all houses come to this.

IN THE STREET OF LOST TIME

Rest and have ease;
Here are no more voyages;
fold, fold your narrow, pale
hands; and under the veil
of night lie, as I have seen you lie
in your deep hair; but patiently
now that new loves, new days,
have gone their ways.

Note
This poem was set to music by Gustav Holst in 1929.

PANTALOON

When Time assails man's citadel and death
   blows the last trumpet, shaking roof and rafter,
music and verse, beauty's deliberate breath,
   shatter the gloom with man's immortal laughter.

HUMORESQUE
ACT I, SCENE I. – PIERROT BLAMES PIERRETTE
From THE STAGE MANAGER

You have the place, the time, the characters.
  These were the perfect lovers, and did not know it,
For Pierrot was a lover in his verse,
  And in her love Pierrette became a poet.

Note
There is an autobiographical touch here, for Humbert's wife, Jessie, did begin writing poetry after their marriage. This is my favourite. MC.

TO A PAINTED HORSE FROM SWEDEN
by Jessie Wolfe (Unpublished)

Sometimes in my room I sit
Quietly, and look at it—
Rows, and rows, and rows of books
Give me many coloured looks,
China cups and saucers dare
Calmly back at me to stare.
Love on tiptoe, posed for flight,
Stays instead for my delight,
And the quiet arm I have found
Like soft arms about me wound.
Now a strange thing has come,
Small and painted, bright, but dumb,
Far across the sea he came.
And I do not know his name.
Fierce he looks and red and bold
But his heart, I fear is cold.
All the Valkyries are fled
And the Vikings long since dead—

Likeness of the steeds of kings,
Now one of my quiet things—
In my room where I sit
Quietly, and look at it.

THE LAMP IN THE EMPTY ROOM

I looked back suddenly into the empty room,
and saw the lamp that I had lit
still shining on the little table by the window,
and throwing its light on the tumbled sheets of paper
on which I had been writing.
And I felt as though long years ago
a man, whom I had known very little,
had lighted that lamp, and sat by the window
writing and believing that he was a poet,
and then he came out of the room and found the letter.
He will not go into the room again:
and not he, but I will go in softly
and put out the lamp, and lay aside
the useless paper.

Note
In the drama Pierrette has left Pierrot, leaving a letter ending with the words: "You were yourself. It was enough for verse, but not enough for love. Farewell Pierrot". MC.

BOY IN THE DUSK

I will make a small statue
   of a boy to-day,
that will half look at you
   and half away.

I will have him standing
   in darkness, but
he will be pretending
   that he is not.

I will give him a fiddle,
   and he will not know
that it broke in the middle
   long ago.

His lips will be parted
   as though he smiled
with the broken-hearted
   grace of a child.

And many will wonder,
   and some will ask,
what I mean by my slender
   "Boy in the Dusk."

"Is he beauty deserted?
   Vision betrayed?
Or a love that started,
   and was afraid?"

"Is he love like a ghost
　In the valley of death?
Or youth that is lost
　and remembereth?"

But I will not name him,
　and every man
must find and acclaim him
　as he can.

Since from childish and small things
　the Boy in the Dusk
may flash into all things
　the heart can ask.

Or he may be only
　a small bronze statue
of a boy, who is lonely,
　and looks half at you.

NEITHER MOON NOR CANDLE-LIGHT

If I looked out on any night,
   at the head of the cold dark stair
I could see a little light
   quietly burning there.

Any night, and every night,
   and all the long night through,
neither moon nor candle-light
   but just the light of you.

Sometimes it glimmered in the air,
   sometimes it brushed the floor,
but every night I found it there;
   I shall not any more.

TIMES

MORNING

In the deep blue
  of heaven mark!
a cloud no bigger
  than a lark.

And hear! against
  your window-pane
his music vertical
  as rain.

Dare we go out,
  and face his song?
I do not think so.
  I was wrong

to walk beneath
  your window thus.
He does not sing this year
  for us.

AUTUMN

RESIGNATION

Come! let us draw the curtains,
  heap up the fire, and sit
hunched by the flame together,
  and make a friend of it.

Listen! the wind is rising,
  and the air is wild with leaves,
we have had our summer evenings:
  now for October eves!

The great beech-trees lean forward,
  and strip like a diver. We
had better turn to the fire,
  and shut our minds to the sea,

where the ships of youth are running
  close-hauled on the edge of the wind,
with all adventure before them,
  and only the old behind.

Love and youth and the seabirds
  meet in the stormy weather,
and with one bright flash of laughter
  clap into the dark together.

Come! let us draw the curtains,
  and talk of other things,
and presently all will be quiet—
  love, youth, and the sound of wings.

DEATH OF HARLEQUINADE

Pierrot with his face of china
very like the ghost of Heine,
when he made his little songs
out of love's enormous wrongs,
trips across the stage, and goes
to a tune upon his toes,
softly keeping time, till he
slips into eternity,
following but missing yet
the dancing shadow of Pierrette.
Pantaloon's too stiff to stir,
but at last the Officer
takes him by the arm, and they
pass together from the play.
Wherefore weep, since all things must
have a common end in dust,
whether late with one, or soon
with another, Pantaloon.
Pierrot will, bemused by pain,
find the dust makes all things plain,
and he will in turn forget,
and be forgotten by Pierrette.
None will heed the Constable.
Dust will choke the prison-bell,
when the wicked and the just
lie together in the dust.
And when all the rest are in
death, the spangled Harlequin,
will himself lie down, and rust,
quiet in the quiet dust.

And whate'er the play may be,
farce, or ancient tragedy,
the poet does not care, who must
with the play himself be dust.

THE FOOL HAS SAID IN HIS HEART

The fool has said in his heart, "There is no God,"
the fool, that proves by mathematics that he is wiser
than the God who invented him and mathematics,
than the God as visible in a division sum
as in the ravishing division of the lute,
the wise fool, that loves nothing but his folly
in which there is no God.
But God has said in His heart, "There is no fool,"
and the fool, and his mathematics, and his fourth dimension are not.
But there is another fool, and older fool than Jaques in Arden,
the pale fool that some call Pierrot, and others call
lads-love, that grows in England in the hedges,
and that fool has said in his heart, "There is no death,"
the fool who throws the golden feather of his love
to drift upon the air, but somewhere a king-eagle
has in the mountain-tops fashioned his eyrie
out of gold feathers, and soaring on the wind
this last and smallest feather finds the nest,
and the king-eagle hides it with his wings.
And death has said in his heart, "There is no fool"
but the scarlet wild anemone and the blue grape hyacinth
blossom each spring in the valley, yes! and climb to the edge of the snows,
and two or three perhaps, sturdier than all their sisters,
find a little cranny underneath the eagle's eyrie,
and one morning when the king-eagle
rises, as though he were tumbling upwards into a star,

he sees, trembling beside his smallest golden feather
the scarlet wild anemone and the blue grape hyacinth.
For this fool has said in his heart, "There is no death,"
and he is right.

Note
Wolfe repeated this poem two years later in *This Blind Rose*, changing the first and last lines to the biblical "The fool hath said".

From NEWS OF THE DEVIL

"War! devil! There is something I remember
out of the world in which I lived. September
through all the fields of France with apple and corn
drifted and dreamed. Morn followed dew-rich morn
with gradual wealth, and the soft silver eves
played Harlequin across the golden leaves.
And while the immemorial harvester
garnered her sheaves, a shadow followed her,
and as she, smiling, whispered 'It is good,'
out of the air a hellish multitude
leaped at her shoulder, yelling as they tore,
'Murder and blood! The harvest-home of war.'
Listen! I can remember something else
I wrote of this, 'War has its miracles
of high regeneration and release
more than the milky benefits of peace.
Men find their souls in battle, having lost them,
nations their hearts, whatever war may cost them.
Strike for the right! Let everything go in.
One touch of murder makes the whole world kin.'
These things I wrote. Outside my window went
on steady feet a marching regiment.
I threw aside the curtain. Shrill and airy
they piped 'The long, long way to Tipperary,'
the short, short way to death,...

From NEWS OF THE DEVIL

And now the devil's voice rose up and out,
like the last trumpet in an army's rout.
"Dust are the stars, and mankind's deepest lust
only a lazy wind that stirs the dust,
and dies again, leaving the dust as level
whether it blew from God or from the devil.
And neither God nor devil knows or cares
how dust may regulate its grey affairs,
since what men call the devil, and their sense
of God, is mankind's last impertinence.
This is self-knowledge, Arthur. Say you sinned,
it is the same as goodness in the end.
What shall it matter if a grain of dust
fulfils its mission or its interest,
since all its interest or mission is,
starting with nameless dust, to end with this?
And say one grain of dust dominion gains
over a thousand, no a myriad grains,
it is no more than if a raindrop tried
shoreward to drag the whole Atlantic tide.
It does not change the other grains, or even
change its own doom, not made in Hell or Heaven,
but in the long decay of the first thought
that slowly crumbles backward into naught.
Grain rubs on grain, and as they work and fester,
contemptuous Time, unconscious, pricks the blister,
God is not mocked, Paul Arthur, by the dust,
and you will mingle quiet with the rest,
as indistinguishable and as small
as though you had not lived or died at all.

Be not afraid, all that you were, and are,
is but the putrefaction of a star,
and nothing that you could have done, or can,
could change the grovelling destiny of man."

Then something in Paul Arthur rose to cry
"I know you, devil, and I know you lie ...."

EPILOGUE

I have sung of love. I am feign of
   love that I cannot sing,
love that is cleansed from the stain of
   the heart's imagining:

Not the love of living and being
   not my own love to me,
but the quiet overseeing
   of man by eternity.

There is a silence folded
   within the heart of peace,
and there our Time is moulded
   into the curve of these.

There is no need for anger,
   there is no cause for pain,
and love's enchanting danger
   bewitches there in vain.

And the music, we had made of
   a whisper and a guess,
will there be unafraid of
   its own full loveliness.

No more as here encumbered
   between the heart and wit,
between the thought remembered,
   and song that failed of it,

between the beauty waiting
   on eyes that dared not see,
and vision hesitating
   on immortality,

But one with what love sings of,
   and one with love that sings,
the soul will touch the strings of
   the harp of which the strings

are chords of light revealing
   the vision absolute,
where love surpasses feeling,
   and song fulfilled is mute.

INVOCATION

FOR
MY DAUGHTER
ANN

Children, there is a lady, who
is younger far than all of you,
who played your games, before you played them,
with Cain and Abel, when they made them,
and who will play them to the end
with the last child, and his last friend.
You do not know her name, nor will,
but you may hear, when all is still,
between the trample of this verse
a quiet footstep that is hers.

PREFACE

The reason why this book is verse
(and nothing, I admit, is worse)
is that, as every schoolboy knows,
it takes much longer to write prose.

P.S.
If someone tries to make you learn it,
just take the beastly book, and burn it.

INTRODUCTION

I

They tell me, children,
    you have some
fugitive Elysi-
    um

where, while your baffled
    elders pass
through what to them is
    common grass,

you walk in fields,
    where never fell
or snow or rain, through
    asphodel.

It may be so. I pray
    it is.
But I at least re-
    member this,

that I myself, when
    I was seven,
instead of wandering
    in heaven,

insisted most
    whole-heartedly
on being nothing else
    than me,

and liked the daisy
    most, because
it went on being
    what it was.

And therefore if to
    me the sun
is just a means
    of waking one,

and if to starshine
    I prefer
the polish on a
    banister,

and is I play my
    private game
of being constantly
    the same

(which is the circumstance
    that wrings
my heart in ordinary
    things),

don't think that
    I am trying to
write, as though I
    were one of you,

or writing (which is
    even worse)
what I suppose a
    child prefers.

I have no views. I only
        know
that fifty thousand
        years ago

the things I write of
        were not new.
That's why I like them. But
        will you?

INTRODUCTION

II

Nor, children, would
    I have you think
I rub my spectacles,
    and blink,

or murmur whimsically
    abject
apologies, when
    you're the subject

of conversation.
    No! I've found
that children, taking
    them all round,

are not the least
    bit better than
their parents. And
    indeed I can

remember some, that
    I would gladly
have smothered, when they
    slammed doors madly,

or when they shouted
    down the stairs,
or badgered me
    with their affairs,

or went on asking
    me the time,
or got their beastly
    dogs to climb

upon my knee, and shed
    their coat
all over me, and what
    I wrote.

While others simply
    are the plan
to which life draws
    a gentleman.

For, with the infant,
    as the grown-up,
the truth, if we're prepared
    to own up,

is that it takes all
    sorts to be
a schoolroom, or a
    nursery,

though possibly there's
    nothing quite
so ineradicably
    right

as children who
    enchant the air
(like Ann) by
    merely being there.

I warn you, therefore,
    if you look
for adulation
    in this book,

or for an attitude
    of dim
belief that you are
    seraphim,

or for a poet who is
    handing
out sweet, indulgent
    understanding,

you will not find it.
    All you'll find
is something I have had
    in mind

since I was six. And
    if it's rotten,
it only shows that I've
    forgotten.

THE BLUECOAT BOY

I

I met an angel in the Strand
with an umbrella in his hand,
talking with Paradisal joy
to a bewildered Bluecoat boy.
"And so," he said, "I understand
this also is a Golden Strand,
that has, like heaven, for example,
an edifice they call the Temple,
and leads by such another Bar
as ours to where the glories are
of what they tell me would be witty
to name the Uncelestial City.
Well! well! Let us examine it."
And, while he spoke, the street was lit
with some strange glory. Tired faces
shone like the sun in country places;
and people's voices sounded, when
they spoke, like chords by Beethoven;
the motor-buses had the hot
splendour of a chariot;
the houses by the Aldwych were
as arrogant as Lucifer;
the island-churches, like a crowd
of golden starlings, cried aloud,
till none could say which were the bells,
and which were simply miracles;
the very paving-stones were led,
enchantingly astonishéd,
into a crazy pattern, laid
to trap the moss in ambuscade.

Indeed the whole excited town
glowed like a shy, delicious noun,
when some great poet lets it live
at last beside its adjective.

And then I saw, like a superb
hawker, the angel at the curb
set London working like a toy—
and give it to the Bluecoat boy.

Note
Bluecoat Boys from Christ's Hospital wearing their Elizabethan dress, a long blue belted coat and yellow stockings, used to be quite a common sight in London, especially near their school in the City; but the school has now moved to the country. MC.

THE SOLDIER

I

Down some cold field in a world unspoken
  the young men are walking together, slim and tall,
and though they laugh to one another, silence is not
    broken:
  there is no sound however clear they call.

They are speaking together of what they loved in vain
    here,
  but the air is too thin to carry the thing they say.
They were young and golden, but they came on pain
    here,
  and their youth is age now, their gold is grey.

Yet their hearts are not changed, and they cry to one
    another,
  "What have they done with the lives we laid aside?
Are they young with our youth, gold with our gold, my
    brother?
  Do they smile in the face of death, because we died?"

Down some cold field in a world uncharted
  the young seek each other with questioning eyes.
They question each other, the young, the golden-
    hearted,
  of the world that they were robbed of in their quiet
    Paradise.

THE RESPECTABLE WOMAN

I

They are singing, but I have not listened
  in the open spaces in spring.
Their white feet in the dances have hastened,
  but mine are not hastening.

They have loosed their hair that is golder
  than laburnum's gold in May,
and the birch in the rain is their shoulder—
  but I have looked away.

They have bound their breasts with rushes,
  they have dived in the forest lake,
but the foot of the satyr crushes
  the lilied reeds in the brake.

The sound of a flute drifts over,
  (but I have closed my ears)
and the air is sweet with the lover,
  and the cry of the fugitive years.

I have not heard nor seen them,
  I have not danced nor sung,
and when love passed between them
  he left my heart unwrung.

They have wasted their lives by spending,
  and are with death rewarded,
but I shall find no ending
  of the life that I have hoarded.

I saved the source of living,
    Thou knowest at what cost,
and, therefore, All-forgiving,
    now give me what I lost!

THE TEACHER
II

They murmur, the children, like bees in summer
   in a hot garden, like bees in a cup,
and, like light through branches, now gay, now dimmer,
   thought touches a face that is lifted up.
My bees, with the pollen under your feet,
   when the thought we shared is no longer alive,
will aught that we dreamed of together be sweet,
   will there be honey of ours in the hive?
It is dark in the hive. There is fear, there is shame,
   there are tears, and ugliness unto death.
Sweet thieves of the sun, must it still be the same,
   or will not the flowers you rifled bequeathe
a glimpse of the vision you saw at my knees,
when the teacher was taught by the Keeper of Bees?

Note
It is interesting to compare this poem with the following extract from HW's *The Uncelestial City*, Book I. Approach to the City; II. Some Advantages of Oxford; II. Over the Fire.

"And teaching is impossible unless,
   like Heine's Northern fir under the false calm
of snow, a self-appointed loneliness
   creates the desert and the weaving palm.

There must be vicarious joy, and the sacrifice
   of one's own summer for an unshared spring,
and to start the migrant swallows before the ice
   back to their South, and never to stir a wing.

At best a kind of sainthood, and at worst
   a drudgery, whose squalid hopes and fears
change what had seemed a martyrdom at first
   into a gradual argument for Squeers."

THE UNCOMMON MAN

I

The feathers in a fan
are not so frail as man;
the green embosséd leaf
than man is no more brief.
His life is not so loud
as the passing of a cloud;
his death is quieter
than harebells, when they stir.
The years that have no form
and substance are as warm,
and space has hardly less
supreme an emptiness.
And yet man being frail
does on himself prevail,
and with a single thought
can bring the world to naught,
as being brief he still
bends to his fleeting will
all time, and makes of it
the shadow of his wit.
Soundless in life and death
although he vanisheth,
the echo of a song
makes all the stars a gong.
Cold, void, and yet the grim
darkness is hot with him,
and space is but the span
of the long love of man.

CODA

THE HIGH SONG

The high song is over. Silent is the lute now.
  They are crowned for ever and discrowned now.
Whether they triumphed or suffered they are mute now,
  or at the most they are only a sound now.

The high song is over. There is none to complain now.
  No heart for healing, and none to break now.
They have gone, and they will not come again now.
  They are sleeping at last, and they will not wake
    now.

The high song is over. And we shall not mourn now.
  There was a thing to say, and it is said now.
It is as though all these had been unborn now,
  it is as though the world itself were dead now.

The high song is over. Even the echoes fail now;
  winners and losers—they are only a theme now,
their victory and defeat a half-forgotten tale now;
  and even the angels are only a dream now.

There is no need for blame, no cause for praise now.
  Nothing to hide, to change or to discover.
They were men and women. They have gone their
    ways now,
  as men and women must. The high song is over.

Note
I heard this poem first at the poetry reading in memory of Humbert Wolfe in February 1940. MC.

THE HOUSE OF GHOSTS

First to describe the house. Who has not seen it
　once at the end of an evening's walk—the leaves
that suddenly open, and as sudden screen it
　with the first flickering hint of shadowy eaves?

Was there a light in the high window? Or
　only the moon's cool candle palely lit?
Was there a pathway leading to the door?
　Or only grass and none to walk on it?

And surely someone cried, "Who goes there—who?"
　And ere the lips could shape the whispered "I,"
the same voice rose, and chuckled, "You, 'tis you!"
　A voice, or the furred night-owl's human cry?

Who has not seen the house? Who has not started
　towards the gate half-seen, and paused, half-fearing,
and half beyond all fear—and the leaves parted
　again, and there was nothing in the clearing?

THIS BLIND ROSE

As this blind rose, no more than a whim of the dust,
   achieved her excellence without intent,
so man, the casual sport of time and lust,
   plans wealth and war, and loves by accident.

A LITTLE MUSIC

Since it is evening,
   let us invent
love's undiscovered
   continent.

What shall we steer by,
   having no chart
but the deliberate
   fraud of the heart?

How shall we find it?
   Beyond what keys
of boyhood's Spanish
   piracies,

false Eldorados
   dim with the tears
of beauty, the last
   of the buccaneers?

Since it is evening,
   let us design
what shall be utterly
   yours and mine.

There will be nothing
   that ever before
beckoned the sailor
   from any shore.

Trees shall be greener
   by mountains more pale,
thrushes outsinging
   the nightingale,

flowers now butterflies,
   now in the grass,
suddenly quiet
   as painted glass,

and fishes of emerald
   dive for the moon,
whose silver is stained by
   the peacock lagoon.

Since it is evening,
   and sailing weather,
let us set out for
   the dream together;

set for the landfall,
   where love and verse
enfranchise for ever
   the travellers.

Note
This poem was set to music by Gustav Holst in 1929.

MOUNTAIN-FLOWERS

Climb by the path, and you'll find mountain-mallow,
   narcissus, restless in the wind, as though
she heard a voice beseech her bloom to follow,
   and softly drown in the reflective snow.

Or higher still, like little red macaws,
   in green sequestered cages, brooding, see!
the Alpine rose, obedient to the laws
   which rule that vertical mute aviary.

Then, last of all, only the edelweiss,
   not soft like any other flower else,
but a small cuttle-fish against the ice,
   clutching the rock with pale grey tentacles.

These and a thousand others, how small, how brittle,
   how easily pulled, how folded in the hand,
and how long afterwards a single petal
   is all we keep of vision's Oberland.

MY POEMS

As always when he has finished writing,
he who takes the pencil out of my hand
looks at me with bright, half-wondering malice,
and says, "Another poem by Humbert Wolfe.
Well, take your poem, and make the most of it!"
And at first, as I read the poem,
it is not my poem at all.
If it is a poem of mountains, it is as tall
and lovely as the mountains themselves.
There will be flowers (O gentians! O gentians!
I saw you in sheets of blue, and I did not know your
   name,
but I said to myself, as a man says
when he sees the face of the chosen woman,
"This is for me and I for this,"
O gentians!)
Or, if it is a poem of life, then like a meadow,
under trees in moonlight, life lies, all dreaming
and still, save for the little moving shadow
of wings between the meadow and the moon.
But presently, as I read,
the words lose their dew, the green
and fragrant thoughts are gradually cloaked
with the dust of the common road
that all feet tread.
And the poem is just a poem like any other
that I have written.
And I give it a name, and sign it, reluctantly,
Humbert Wolfe.

But the true poem—the one that I have not written,
of which mine is the discarded husk,
is safe with him who wrote it,
and with the poets who, when this stranger smiled,
caught him by the wing, and, though they could not
  hold him,
found in their star-stained hands one golden feather,
which touched their page.

GENEVA
I. RUE DU SOLEIL LEVANT

There is no sun that rises anywhere
as reticent as in St. Peter's Square,
till his slow torrent negligently reaches
the slanting thoroughfare behind the beeches,
down which he plunges in a racing flood
to drench the town below with golden mud.
But, when his tide has ebbed, the river-bed
looks back to Calvin with a hint of red,
to shew that you remember how you won
your name, small sister of the rising sun.

SPRING WOOD

I wish that I could go back
to Spring Wood below Hawksworth—yes!
I wish I might sleep, and wake
under the branches of those loved trees.
But Bradford lies far away,
and the wood beyond Bradford far;
and never between night and day,
not under sun, nor cool star,
shall I go back to Bradford,
to Spring Wood below Hawksworth Hall.
There is no way back at evening;
there is no way back at all.

NOW IN THESE FAIRYLANDS

Now in these fairylands
gather your weary hands
close to your breast,
and be at rest.

Now in these silences
lean to the cadences,
moulding their grace
to the line of your face.

Now at the end of all,
loveliest friend of all,
all things are yours,
in this peace that endures.

Note
This poem was set to music by Gustav Holst in 1929.

THE UNCELESTIAL CITY
BOOK I. APPROACH TO THE CITY
From I. MR. CRAYFISH DISCUSSES HIS SON'S FUTURE WITH HIS CONSCIENCE

"Do you know Blackford? Nature keeps the tally
of those who found a smooth embosomed valley,
waiting for dawn among her hills, and splendid
with the shadow of her trees when day was ended,
who found this valley, and, being business-men,
swore that these things should not occur again.
They therefore added up a maze of brick
by some unspeakable arithmetic,
quietly boasting, as they clinched the sum,
God makes the country, but we make the slum…

THE UNCELESTIAL CITY
BOOK I. APPROACH TO THE CITY
THE FIDDLER

If I had money, as I have none,
I'd buy the City, and sell it for fun
to a little black pig, who a long time since
started life as a fairy prince.
And while the others were all for trough,
he was over the hills and a long way off
catching the moon, and letting a star go
that was caught in the top'sle rig of his Argo.
And he swore, as he sailed out with the tide,
he would see death's eyes on the other side.
And he steered for the sun, like a baby feeling
there must be some way up the wall to the ceiling,
and the stippled clouds in a long low frieze
were the fairy-tale of the Golden Fleece.
But alas! gold apples, alas! dream's high land!
there lies a green enchanted island,
where Circe claims the heart for hers
even of beauty's moonrakers.
And the fleece is lost, and the clouds are cold,
and there is no gold but fairy gold,
fairy gold that tumbles and splashes
into the water, dust and ashes.
And the deeper it plunges, the deeper they dig
this little pig, and that little pig.
"Grunt," says the first, and "Grunt," says his brother,
and each one gravely approves the other.
And as for the sty, it becomes, as they stir,
muddier and muddier.

But, it may be, Odysseus, that ancient wizard,
will catch my swine, and slit up his gizzard.
And the sty will blossom with olive and quince,
and the hog will be walking there straight as a prince.

THE UNCELESTIAL CITY
BOOK I. APPROACH TO THE CITY
II. SOME ADVANTAGES OF OXFORD
From II. OVER THE FIRE

You cannot hope
  to bribe or twist,
thank God! the
  British journalist.

But, seeing what
  the man will do
unbribed, there's
  no occasion to."

THE UNCELESTIAL CITY
BOOK I. APPROACH TO THE CITY
II. SOME ADVANTAGES OF OXFORD
From II. OVER THE FIRE

'The primrose on
　the river's brim
was one-and-six a
　line to him.

And though he grumbled,
　begged, and swore
(believe me) it was
　nothing more.'

THE UNCELESTIAL CITY
BOOK I. APPROACH TO THE CITY
II. SOME ADVANTAGES OF OXFORD
From II. OVER THE FIRE

"Eve heard you singing,
   and rippled 'Hark,
God is amused! Oh,
   What a lark!'"

"And Adam answered,
   'Eve, you've said it,'
but naturally
   took the credit

of having been the
   first who heard
all heaven laughing
   in a bird."

Which written, Jobson
   went near by
to lunch on lark and
   oyster pie.

Which makes me wonder
   whether He,
Jobson, who made the
   lark made thee.'

THE UNCELESTIAL CITY
BOOK I. APPROACH TO THE CITY
II. SOME ADVANTAGES OF OXFORD
From II. OVER THE FIRE

'The House of Lords
  are waiting for
the newspaper
  proprietor.

Soap! Attention!
  Listen! Beer!
"Glory to the
  new-made peer."

Hark! the Heralds'
  College sings,
as they fake his
  quarterings.'

THE UNCELESTIAL CITY
BOOK I. APPROACH TO THE CITY
II. SOME ADVANTAGES OF OXFORD
From II. OVER THE FIRE

'Up and down Pall Mall, and then
   back to Piccadilly,
educated gentlemen,
   exquisitely silly,
sit about, and lounge about,
   talking, eating, drinking,
and the only thing they do without
   (I understand) is thinking.'

THE UNCELESTIAL CITY
BOOK I. APPROACH TO THE CITY
IV.
THE FIDDLER
FAREWELL TO YOUTH

Agamemnon sleeps at last in Argos.
   Be still, nightingales. No king
will marshal the long ships now
   by the sand-beaches. Why do you sing?

Achilles is fleet of foot no longer.
   Hector is the dust of a moth's wing,
and the great shield is tarnished.
   Argive nightingales, why do you sing?

It is over, Agamemnon, Agamemnon,
   the Iliad of our youth and of spring.
Oh, why do men love like heroes;
   and nightingales! why do you sing?

THE UNCELESTIAL CITY
BOOK III. SCENES IN THE CITY
I. MR CRAYFISH WALKS HOME FROM THE COURTS
SPRING IN LONDON I.

"When all the London boys begin
with one accord their tops to spin,
when girls through last year's rubbish grope
for what looks like a skipping-rope,
when even babies turn from croup
to tumble with a wooden hoop,
and minnows tremble at the string—
then London trembles into spring.

When motor-buses, eastward stepping,
make the distant port of Epping,
when taxis give a single snort
and find themselves at Hampton Court,
when every lover and his lass
go Underground to Lyonesse—
then costermongers' barrows bring
—yellow and white—the London spring.

When every Round Pond goose is chuckling
at the perfection of her duckling,
and two grey cygnets make the swan
the proudest bird in Kensington,
when the fresh water stings like brine
the gulls along the Serpentine,
and every sparrow has his fling—
your ludship, that's the London spring."

Notes
These ducks are geese enough to think their ugly ducklings cygnets. MC.

THE UNCELESTIAL CITY
BOOK III. SCENES IN THE CITY
I. MR CRAYFISH WALKS HOME FROM THE COURTS
WORMWOOD SCRUBS

"I think there must be some
black magic in the drum!
For the fiddle, the flute, and the brass
stir in the heart, and pass
with a flicker of flowers or wings.
But dark and different things
mutter in the drum, and crack
into the soul like a black
ghost in a garden of white
hollyhocks, haunting by night.

I have heard fiddles shrilly
sweet in Piccadilly,
when London life goes past in spring
like Mrs. Siddons curtseying.

And in the copper-beeches
at Kew a flute beseeches
with her single argent glimmer
of delight the London summer.

Yes! and the golden shout
of brass is all about
winter, with a fire lit,
and all London warm at it.

Fiddle to fiddle, flute to flute
answer, and with the brass are mute.
But all the time, as soft as sleep,
dark, continual, and deep,
ebbing, flowing, parting, meeting,
as though he were your own heart beating,
a sullen distant drummer drubs,
'Youth and spring in Wormwood Scrubs.'"

THE UNCELESTIAL CITY
BOOK IV. SCENES IN THE CITY
II. MR. CRAYFISH, K.C., AND CONTEMPORARY YOUTH
From OVER THE FIRE

You can fool life perhaps at twenty-one,
   at twenty-five still treat it as a topic,
but after that the farce will lose its fun,
    and, whether you like it or not, become an epic.

THE UNCELESTIAL CITY
BOOK IV. THE END OF THE PATH
CAPITAL PUNISHMENT
THE FIDDLER

It is easier to be angry than to pity,
   it is easier to condemn than to understand,
easier to find the Uncelestial City
   than the dim counties of the Holy Land.

I too have raged, I too have sullenly rated,
   I too have judged men being judged by these.
And I have loved far less than I have hated,
   and was proud of this, like all the Pharisees.

Shall I not, therefore, now that the day is over,
   remember, if men sinned, that they have suffered,
come back at nightfall an unfaithful lover,
   who would not understand the love they offered?

Shall I not see that to live is to have relinquished
   beauty to the sequestration of the dark,
and yet that the spirit of man, benighted, vanquished
   has folded wings, and shall use them as the lark

into the sun beyond the cold clouds flinging
   her desperate hope, not reaching where she has
     striven,
but soaring for ever beyond herself, and singing
   high above earth as she is low in heaven?

Shall I not confess that mine own evil humour
   and not man's failure forged this black despair,
and, while I wept, high up the golden rumour
   of the lark ascending fringed the quiet air?

Oh, I will listen to that, and, when I falter,
   hold up my hands above me in my blindness,
you ancient virtues, man's immortal shelter,
   faith, and the courage to fail in all but kindness.

Hold up my hands! And, while the battle sways
   beneath the least of the watchers on the hill,
let me remember that, though my heart betrays
   the cause of man, you are his angels still;

that, while you watch, although the night descend,
   you uphold it in your hands, like the silk woof
of some black Sultan's palanquin, and bend
   it vastly over the head of man for a roof

powdered with stars, and with the moon for a lamp,
   confronting God, rejoinder to the tomb,
giving the soul of man, though the last trump
   blare through the curtains, the right to his own
                     room.

THE UNCELESTIAL CITY
BOOK V. RETORT BY MRS. JAKES
(MORTE SMITH)
V.
THE MOON AND MRS. SMITH

Pausing in her cool affairs,
through the basement window stares
moon, and with cold witcheries
makes a drypoint out of mess...
Dishes in her silver pool
almost glimmer beautiful;
meat, torn papers, broken knife,
glitter with a secret life;
even the taps that splash and sprawl
become a lunar waterfall.
Last her pencils touch the chair
with a sly and dexterous air.
Face, clasped hands, and unshrugged
  shoulder
placid silver. Moon grows bolder,
inscribes her tranquil etching with,
"Life and death of Mrs. Smith."

X AT OBERMMERGAU
Part I. TAIL-PIECE
THE REGULAR CHORUS
(ENDING THEIR DAY'S REHEARSAL)

Fades now the star, and, by their camels kneeling
   framed in the doorway where the dawn engages
their coloured silks with deeper colour stealing
   out of the East triumphant, stands the Mages
     with bended brow
world without end to-day at Oberammergau.

Note
HW saw the Passion Play at Oberammergau in 1930. He, my mother and I, stayed in the house of Melchior Breitsampter, who was playing Pontius Pilate. As a Roman, he was one of the few clean-shaven men in Oberammergau. AW.

X AT OBERMMERGAU
From PART II. TAIL PIECE
MARY MOTHER LEADS THE CHORUS

He has gone down to death. Cease, women, your sorrow.
  There is naught for you to lament and naught to cry on.
He has taken death under his arm like an arrow
  whose barb is broken. Lift up your gates, O Zion.
      The bacon burns
beyond the world. He is risen. Christ returns.

THE UPWARD ANGUISH

From CHAPTER I: SCHOLARSHIP JOURNEY

It began when, at the age of seventeen, he stepped into a Great Northern railway carriage with a third-class return ticket to Oxford in his pocket. Nobody supposed that he would get his Scholarship that year. He had, moreover, signalized the approaching ordeal by a bilious attack. His nose divided a yellow, though plump, face with the emphasis which marked his frequent periods of ill-health. But he did not greatly care. They might think that he would need a second try. He knew better. His Latin and Greek were, admittedly, moderate, but let the heroes from Eton and Harrow beat him at English if they could. They were heartily invited to try.

He had a new coat and white woollen gloves, the latter acquired because he had learned that they were the Oxford fashion of the moment. His coat had been approved by his Form master and he had been adjured not to think of the exam during the journey. "Your chance is freshness," he had been told, "and a sort of inspired cheek." "Cheek doesn't go down everywhere," he replied, thinking of an episode in Lister Park a couple of years before when two older boys had stopped him in order to tell him that he was a conceited and, therefore, ridiculous young fool, and would be blackballed for the School Literary Society. He was.

He remembered the episode as he sat in his corner in the train, wondering whether a cigarette would make him sick. He took out his packet, looking round to see whether his air of a confirmed smoker had impressed his travelling-companions. They did not seem much moved. He re-pocketed the unused Golden Stars and reflected upon Newsham and Arthur—his assailants. They had had him blackballed, but they could not prevent his becoming a member when he reached the Sixth at the age of fourteen—in itself a proof both of conceit and cheek. He regretted that, in the aloof splendour which they had attained at Oxford, they did not know that in the winter term he had won the Silver Cup for the best speech of the term. He had vindicated the brilliant military conduct of Sir Redvers Buller, who in the recent Boer War had given the highest indications open to a General. He had lost all his battles, and what more could a soldier do? He wished that those chaps had heard his peroration, which drew, he thought, a neat comparison between Pericles and Cecil Rhodes. "The memorial of a great man," he murmured to himself, "is his City-state. Cecil Rhodes lies buried in the Matoppos. His grave is the British Empire."

He began to scrabble for a pencil. He might have time to finish a poem before he reached Leicester, where he had to change into the Oxford train. But, he thought, I can only write poems at night and in my bedroom looking over to the single light of Scotland Farm on the left and to the line of lights past Peel Park. Besides, I've written a poem this week, and one a week is the allowance prescribed. Still, I'd rather like them to see me writing. It would show that I wasn't in business. And if I spoke the words aloud—as I always do—but even he thought that this was going a little too far. In fact, he had a sensation of blushing at a social folly narrowly escaped. He looked round again, and this time was relieved to discover that nobody had noticed him at all.

At the same time he was a trifle disturbed. Showing off, he

knew, was not the least of his failings, but he hadn't in fact, had he, shown off? And what matter if he had recited to himself the poem entitled "To a Poet Scorned," of which the first verse ran:

> My songs unheard, I come to earth,
>   Darkness I ask, long sleep,
> Why should I pray for second birth
>   who would but wake to weep?

This time he had fairly done it. The business-man opposite had lowered his *Bradford Observer* and was watching him with an amused grin. "It's bright and early," he said, "to be talking to yourself." "I wasn't talking," he replied loftily. "I was reciting." "Ay," he answered, "but it'll do you no good among them chaps at Oxford if they think you're a softie." "How did you know I was going to Oxford?" he enquired. "Seeing that you've had your ticket out ten times and asked porter at Laisterdyke and Halifax wheer to change, it was easy guessing. You're Boogs Wolff, aren't you?" "Yes," he replied defensively, with the air of one who added, "and why not?" "Well then, young Boogs," he said, "don't give yourself away. Sell yourself." He saw at a glance that this was mean commercial advice, but he could find no answer. The man still watched him. "You'll have to try hard," he said. "It won't be none too easy for you." "They don't expect me to get a Scholarship," he replied. "It's not Scholarship I'm meaning," he answered. "You're clever enoof, they say. It's being a Bradford Jew and thinking yourself a nob. Nay," he said, seeing a movement of wounded pride, "Ah'm not meaning to offend you. Just warn you to go slow-like." The train stopped with a rattle of brakes. "Leicester," shouted the porters. As a decisive reply to his impertinent monitor he leaped instantly out of the train—and fell on the platform with his bag. The businessman looked out. "Not hurt?" he said; "Good! but you wouldn't have toombled if you'd gone slower."

AT THE END OF THE AVENUE

I have walked to the end of the avenue,
and there is no figure in the clearing at the end.
It was something in the way that the trees grew:
but I shall pretend
that the evening sunlight falls on a cold
face, and touches the line of the breast
with the last level gold
out of the West.
And since I found it not in all those avenues
on all those other eves,
why should the mind refuse
what the heart believes?

THE LIGHT-FOOTED

See! they are returning
  the light-footed ones—
The midnight grass is burning,
  as each one runs.
Swifter than torches,
  keener than knife!
O, wind in the birches
  it is love pacing life.

THE SNOW-DICTATED PEACE

Once in the life of men
a light clings
about their head as though
God saw again
the swift innumerable wings
of the first snow.
As one who is wakened
to a world redrawn
by the pencil of rime
so, in that second,
dawn
escapes from time.
None can foreknow or prepare
the brilliant slender
moment of release.
It is there.
We surrender
to the snow-dictated peace.

TWO OBOLS

Here are two obols, sailor,
and let you ferry
a phantom paler
than mist in your wherry
till the black unbroken
silence defers
to the dim moth-spoken
passengers.
Pole swift up the river
to put me over
on the shore where never
again for the lover
the veils and the voices
shimmer and lift,
and the heart, that rejoices,
breaks. Boatman, be swift!

Note
This poem is addressed to Charon, the aged ferryman who, in ancient Greek mythology used to ferry dead souls across the rivers of the underworld. He demanded two obols for his services. The Greeks used to stick a two obol coin in the mouths of their corpses. MC.

RED SHOES

Wear your red shoes as once
on such a night, as deep
with blue or bronze
a dark Venetian lady
wore such red shoes.
And that great use
has made your red shoes seem
as though love danced in them
wearing the silken mask,
the flowered domino.
Wear them because I ask—
and when I go.

I PRAISE OTHER WOMEN

I praise other women in you,
not the ladies of legend but
the quiet ones,
the innumerable cohort, who
have heard the gates shut
behind their love or their sons,
and go steadfast on their ways.
These women, praising you, I praise.

HOLLINGS HILL

Last year (a hundred years ago?)
        I walked up Hollings Hill.
I do not know (does any know?)
        if it is climbing still
out of the clatter, out of smoke
        into a quiet place,
where all that cracked or flawed or broke
        resumes its ancient grace,
where with the curlews highly calling,
        and the wind upon the heath,
the benisons of youth are falling
        upon the world beneath,
till ruined hearts, that life has nailed on
        the Cross of their own making,
are lifted down where over Baildon
        the dawn is re-awaking.
Last year (a hundred years ago)
        I heard on Hollings Hill
a world of larks. Does any one know
        if they are singing still?

ANOTHER WAY

There is another way past the brickyard
   past the board school playground and the petrol
     pumps.
You turn by the end of the electric tram-lines,
   between the gasometer and the municipal dumps.

No need to change your ready-made trousers,
   nor wash your celluloid collar, nor trouble
to adjust your slouch, nor straighten your shoulders,
   nor lift your working boots high over the rubble.

There is another way and a woman to walk with.
   See, she points over her shoulder with her thumb.
She looks like a portrait of someone in the papers,
   but don't bother about that or anything, only come!

Those patches on the left are market-gardens,
   advertisements, no doubt, of Mutton's seeds,
and on the right those lawns laid with green damask
   are probably designed for golfers' needs.

Nor let those clouds pretend that they are mountains.
   The wild moraine, the glacier, the peak
are, as you see, an accident of vision,
   a transient, though incandescent, freak.

And that's not music that surpasses Mozart
   with a more magical flute than aught he played with.
It is a flaw of the wind and two late blackbirds,
   or what the wind and the blackbird's song are made
     with.

And you're not young, as you suppose and wearing
   strange silks, nor with a lady at your side
that would have been a princess in Palmyra,
   walking beside her lover as a bride.

O no! she does not wear night for a mantle,
   nor is a star entangled in her tresses,
nor have you words in syllables of fire,
   flame by dark flame, to match dark lovelinesses.

Nor are you two beside that ancient river
   where, like ascending angels, the swans climb,
lovers together in the rose-communion
   of love the flower with her sister Time.

There is another way. O lovely mirage,
   cheat of the heart, we know you what you are,
and still we follow, like the Kings before us,
   because it is impossible, the star.

CONVERSATION GALANTE

Surely it is not you. Sit, nevertheless,
on the wicker-chair where a rag of your dress
was caught, and may, for all I know, be flying
a black signal-flag of the faith that we are denying.
So, sink back in your worn cushions! stretch your hand
with your dim gold air of a conductor, poising his wand
before the first bar of, "The Unfinished". Give the
    rail
the little decisive tap and then, powder-pale,
dim as dead music through lace, softer and dimmer,
let the notes out of smoke driftingly glimmer
into the first chord, that is the rag on the chair,
your outstretched hand, the sea-wrack of your hair
floating backwards on a cold ebb, and the light that dies
in those sconces that were, do you remember, your
    eyes!
So let us talk, though the affable phrases loiter
like news intercepted by an archangelic Reuter
of some vague ancient battle, some uneasy stir
between the unfallen ghosts of love and Lucifer.
"The days draw out." "Really, this English weather."
(So we begin in social voices together.)
"Have you been well - that tiny patch on the lung?"
"Nothing! one can't, you know, be eternally young.
But you? I hear so little these days. Are you still
    writing?"
"What did I use to answer?" "The swans are
    flighting."
"Well they have flown their last." "But whither, and
    why?"
"After many summers (vide Tennyson) even swans
    die!

Slowlier they mount, crying, year after year until
the air over the lake is empty and the wings are still."
"And is there no echo in the heart of the vanished
 wings?"
"The sedge is withered on the lake and no bird sings."
"The Belle dame sans merci." "Where the heart beats
low we are all the knight-at-arms of Keats."
"And she—the sorceress?" "Ah, she discovers
no trace in the dew of any last year's lovers.
Young and unchanging she moves in the teeth of time
safe in the long fidelities of rhyme,
queen of the instant, whose coronation is
the brief and brilliant anguish of the kiss."
"So bitter still!" "If it be bitter to wonder
why the laurel trees are cut with the oleander,
why we walk no more in the woods, where note by note
song's falling fountain matched the blackbird's throat."
"And no way back?" "The shades on Charon's bark
however they may entreat, are for the dark.
And had the gods, like Orpheus, tempted me,
you had not listened, nor followed, Eurydice."

"Then it's good-bye again." Ah, no! at most
the laying by another of a ghost
with the dim echo of a word, once said,
and now by both remembered, being dead.
"But I am keeping you. And there's the bell!"
"No need to rise." "And none to say 'Farewell'."

KING AND CAT

Said the King to the Cat
"What are you looking at?"

"At a mouse shivering
on your throne, O king
      That
is what I am looking at,"
    said the cat.

"Where is the mouse, O cat,
that you are looking at?"

"Do you not feel, O king,
Small, grey and shivering
      what
I am hunting at?"
    said the cat.

"Why draw so near me, that
I feel your cold breath, cat?"

"When the time has come to spring,
death—the old mouser—king
      doth
strike with his icy breath.
    Thus—" the cat saith.

EPITAPH

Now it is time to sleep.
I only ask
to be allowed to keep
unpierced the mask,
behind whose close
and changing covers
I hid myself from foes
      and lovers.

KENSINGTON GARDENS IN WAR-TIME

VI

The woman who used
  to sell in shapes
of large and coloured
  muscat grapes
toy-balloons, has
  left. Instead
vast monsters hover
  overhead,
and why we have to
  play with those,
goodness and Hitler
  only knows.

Note
'Vast monsters' - barrage balloons or 'blimps' which hovered over most of the grass in the parks and open spaces in war-time London. MC.

KENSINGTON GARDENS IN WAR-TIME

VIII

In the Dutch Garden
  (that a man
once wrongly called
  Italian)

the flowers are
  faded. Nothing comes
except the last
  chrysanthemums.

And if you ask
  what gardeners do
all the weary
  winter through,

remember that
  for plants and men
April always
  comes again,

and that the gardener
  plans for this
bright and floral
  Armistice,

as men with heavier
  tasks than these
through war's long winter
  work for peace.

Note
Ignoring the advice of his doctor, my father worked at the Ministry of Labour right up to the time of his death. AW.
"Wrongly called Italian" in a poem in *Kensington Gardens*.

KENSINGTON GARDENS IN WAR-TIME

XV

All along the Broad Walk
listen how the soldiers talk,
ghost to ghost and shade to shade.
"This was where, (I think) we played;
This was where we meant to bring
a girl to match the green of spring;
this was where we said good-bye
to all of that. I can't think why."

KENSINGTON GARDENS IN WAR-TIME

XVI

A man who thirty years ago
   walked in the Gardens and overheard
(he thought and claimed) the feathers grow
   under the elbows of a bird

returns alone to sit and ponder
   under black trees and tries to guess
where was it—here or there or yonder—
   the unrecaptured loveliness,

what was it, beast or bird or flower,
   a voice that spoke or lips that smiled?
O no! you fool, it was her power—
   your lost, but unforgotten, child.

KENSINGTON GARDENS IN WAR-TIME

XVII

They will not come back, the children,
   who used to play on the grass.
It is no good looking
   for what was,

There was one had a coat
   trimmed bravely with fur.
Wherever I seek I
   shall not come up with her.

It is no good hoping
   she will step out from behind a tree.
She is the one thing between earth and heaven
   I shall not see.

KENSINGTON GARDENS IN WAR-TIME

XX

Some people say, and some people think,
that Round Pond water is good to drink,

but others say that you've got to be thin—oh
thinner than that—and svelte as a minnow.

Some people think that the Pond is so small
it isn't a thing you can notice at all.

But one girl, who sat there, found it so wide
that she couldn't see to the other side.

She worked at Smith's, and they called her "Cash",
and her eyes were grey as the drifted ash.

And Jim and she had been gay and fond,
and quarrelled and parted by the Pond.

She sat quite still, but he strode over
the grass, and now, if she looks for her lover,

because of the war, and the way that he died,
she cannot see to the other side.

Note
I find this poem very moving. The first two verses, especially the second, seem strangely incongruous and might have been changed if Wolfe had lived to revise the poem. But I think the poignancy depends on the tragedy growing out of carefree chatter. MC.

KENSINGTON GARDENS IN WAR-TIME

XXX

A solitary Persian cat
observed that she was looking at
the stupid way in which mankind
did all things always front behind.

"Here, for example, is a Park,
clearly intended for the dark,"
she said, "with ample latitude
for stalking and procuring food

according to the ancient law
(vide R. Kipling) of tooth and claw.
Instead of which in Kensington,
when that intrusive oaf—the sun—

has had the decency to quit
what do they do along of it?
So far from realizing that
any self-respecting cat

needs when she drifts, with her tail swishing
silence (as men do when they're fishing)
they rush about in motor-lorries,
enough to frighten all the quarries

in Europe, and they send up beams
of light that does not shine but screams.
And then the people I permit
to share my flat are by with it.

Instead of seeing milk and fish
is set, according to my wish,
and that the maid has brushed my fur,
they read a wretched newspaper,

whose only use is that it slips
easily round the fish and chips.
But there! they will not listen. Hush!
You will forgive me if I rush?"

An air-raid warning? Planes are over?
You (and the mouse) are taking cover.
Let me with Burns remind you then,
'The best-laid plans of mice and men.'"

Index of First Lines

A man who thirty years ago	122
A solitary Persian cat	125
Agamemnon sleeps at last in Argos.	92
Alf and Betty	23
All along the Broad Walk	121
All that I ask	33
And now the devil's voice rose up and out,	54
And you're not young, as you suppose and wearing	114
As always when he has finished writing,	79
As this blind rose, no more than a whim of the dust,	75
Beyond the town—oh far! beyond it	35
Children, there is a lady, who	58
Clean as a lady	16
Climb by the path, and you'll find mountain-mallow,	78
Come! let us draw the curtains,	48
Do you know Blackford? Nature keeps the tally	84
Down some cold field in a world unspoken	68
Eve heard you singing,	89
Fades now the star, and, by their camels kneeling	100
False dreams, all false,	26
First to describe the house. Who has not seen it	74
He has gone down to death. Cease, women, your sorrow.	101
Here are two obols, sailor,	109
I have always known just where the river ends	9
I have sung of love. I am feign of	56
I have walked to the end of the avenue,	106
I looked back suddenly into the empty room,	43
I met an angel in the Strand	66
I praise other women in you,	111
I think there must be some	94
I will make a small statue	44
I wish that I could go back	82

If I had money, as I have none,	85
If I looked out on any night,	46
In the deep blue	47
In the Dutch Garden	120
In the far corner	19
Into spring	15
It is easier to be angry than to pity,	97
It's not my fault, now is it? I'm a Jew.	1
Laburnum hangs	18
Last year (a hundred years ago?)	112
Let's be done with talking,	8
Like a small grey	22
Nor, children, would	63
Now in these fairylands	83
Now it is time to sleep.	118
On a dream-hill we'll build our city,	28
On Betelgeuse	37
Once in the life of men	108
Out! All out!	25
Past Buckhurst Hill the motor-bus	12
Pausing in her cool affairs,	99
Pierrot with his face of china	49
Rest and have ease;	39
Said the King to the Cat	117
Said the old deaf gardener	17
See! they are returning	107
Since it is evening,	76
Some day I'll go back to Oxford—	30
Some people say, and some people think,	124
Sometimes when I think of love	6
Surely it is not you. Sit, nevertheless,	115
The City Financier	20
The feathers in a fan	72
The fool has said in his heart, There is no God,	51

The gold cock-pheasant	24
The high song is over. Silent is the lute now.	73
The House of Lords	90
The little houses in the street	7
The old bellwether	21
The primrose on	88
The reason why this book is verse	59
The sun is shining in the August weather	10
The upper clawses they don't like the smell	3
The woman who used	119
The Yorkshire Grey like any other pub	4
There is another way past the brickyard	113
There is no sun that rises anywhere	81
There's a small café off the Avenue	5
There's someone at the door, said gold candlestick	34
They are singing, but I have not listened	69
They murmur, the children, like bees in summer	71
They tell me, children,	60
They will not come back, the children,	123
This little sleeper, who was overtaken	11
Up and down Pall Mall, and then	91
War! devil! There is something I remember	53
Wear your red shoes as once	110
When all the London boys begin	93
When the house of the heart is empty,	38
When time assails man's citadel and death	40
You can fool life perhaps at twenty-one,	96
You cannot hope	87
You go by motor-bus from Hammersmith	2
You have the place, the time, the characters.	41